DEEPENING
YOUR PRAYER LIFE

GETTING IN TOUCH
WITH THE HEART OF GOD

DEEPENING YOUR PRAYER LIFE

GETTING IN TOUCH
WITH THE HEART OF GOD

Presented By
JILL BRISCOE

Compiled by
SHELLY ESSER

Just Between Us magazine, Brookfield, Wisconsin 53045

DEEPENING YOUR PRAYER LIFE

© 2019 by *Just Between Us* magazine.

Printed in the United States of America

This book is part of a series on relevant topics for *Just Between Us*. For more information on other titles in this series or for information about *Just Between Us* magazine, please turn to the back of this book.

The Team: Allie Alexy, Carol Becwar, Ann Blackburn, Suzan Braun, Debbie Leech, Melinda Papador, and Kelly Perso

Cover Design: Sophie Beck

just between us

DEEPENING YOUR PRAYER LIFE

Why is prayer so hard? We know we need to grow in our prayer life, but it can be such a struggle. And, too often, instead of using it as the first line of defense, we go to it as a last resort. Are you desiring a deeper prayer life? Do you want to get the passion back? If you want to walk in greater victory while enjoying answered prayer on a regular basis, it's time to engage with God on a deeper level. In these 10 chapters, you'll discover how prayer can be one of the greatest adventures of your life— and you'll find prayer strategies to help you in every circumstance you face—while getting in touch with the heart of God.

1

Prayer That Works

Revolutionizing your prayer life.

by Jill Briscoe

Ever since I was a little girl in war-torn England, sitting on a three-legged stool in front of my house waiting for the bombs to fall, I have wanted my prayers to work. I remember praying, "Oh, God, please stop the war." He didn't, and I remember feeling very disappointed with Him. Maybe you have prayed that God would stop the conflict raging around you or in your own life, and He hasn't, and you feel disappointed with Him too. Maybe you feel like your prayers didn't work.

You may wonder what the words *prayer* and *work* are doing in the same sentence. Surely that sounds like an oxymoron! Do you know what an oxymoron is? It's when you put two seemingly contradictory words together, like jumbo shrimp, civil war, or child safe! Prayer and work seem to be opposite concepts. Yet, I have discovered that prayer that doesn't work, doesn't work! It takes work to step out of time into eternity, and work to learn the art of leaving things undone so that the greater thing can be done.

Prayer that works isn't merely a matter of personality or gift, although some people have a propensity for praying or have the gift of prayer (and this gift is something that worries the devil very much. Prayer itself is a gracious gift of God in the sense that He made it possible for us to walk right into His presence and talk to Him as our Father. Every child of God has that right and privilege.

But if Satan has his way, the first thing to go in our devotional life will be our devotional life! As the little couplet says, "The devil trembles when he sees the weakest saint upon his knees." He will do anything to stop us from praying. Sometimes he doesn't have to do anything at all, however, because we assist him by doing away with our prayer life all on our own.

WHEN GOD DOESN'T SEEM TO ANSWER

Often, one of the reasons we stop praying is that we're disappointed with the whole concept of prayer. When we urgently request something from God and He doesn't come through for us, we feel hurt and even betrayed that our prayers have not been answered. That's what happened to me when I was small.

I remember that first urgent attempt to call on the Almighty. The need arose when I became aware that someone was trying to kill me! The Second World War was in full swing and I had the misfortune to live in Liverpool, a dangerous place. Ships supplying us with food from our allies brought their precious cargo to this seaport, making it a target for the enemy. I was very young, but I was aware that there was a God in heaven, and somewhere deep down in my heart I knew He was perfectly capable of stopping wars and conflicts. I decided one day that I would ask Him to stop these terrible airplanes from dropping bombs all over my life.

That night the air raids were particularly vicious. While we were huddled in our underground shelter like little moles, I confidently asked God to intervene. The answer came immediately: The bomb dropped far too near for comfort, damaging the back of our house, and sending us running for shelter. *What went wrong?* I asked myself furiously, trying in my six-year-old mind to make sense out of this nonsense. Had God not heard? Had I said my prayer with the wrong words or in the wrong way? Then came the unwelcome thought:

Perhaps God didn't hear me because He was too busy doing other things like keeping the stars in place. And last came the worst thought: *Maybe He couldn't help me because he couldn't help me. He wasn't big enough or strong enough.*

One way or another my fervent request had been ignored, and a huge sense of betrayal gripped me. Somewhere deep down in my six-year-old heart I determined not to try again. Not a few adults have faced similar dilemmas. At the first disappointment they quit without finding out what is happening and what makes prayer work.

If this is the case, the first thing we should do is pray about this. In fact, we should pray about anything that hinders our prayer life. You might want to stop this moment and ask the Lord to identify whatever has caused you to stop talking to Him. Then, when you have an inkling of what the blockage has been, talk to Him about it.

MASTER THE ART OF LEAVING THINGS UNDONE

The first thing you need to learn as you begin to pray prayers that work is to master the art of leaving things undone. Many of us suffer from "Martha syndrome." Martha was a woman who loved Jesus very much, but her "much serving" distracted her from focusing on Him (Luke 10:40, NKJV). It's hard to leave the urgent thing to attend to one's soul, but the Lord calls us to just such a duty. You have to learn to do it in the middle of the muddle! Martha had good reasons not to sit at Jesus' feet, but those reasons were not enough for the Lord. He said to her, "Martha, Martha... you are worried and upset about many things, but only one thing is needed. Mary has chosen what is better, and it will not be taken away from her" (Luke 10:41-42, NKJV). Many of us can get so excited about the work of the Lord that we forget the Lord of the work, as someone has so aptly said.

SIMPLY GET STARTED

But where do we start when we meet with God? One of the reasons some people avoid personal devotions is a fear of incompetence. *Whatever shall we say when we enter His throne room?* They wonder. Maybe we've always had a problem talking to important people. How do you address the King of Kings and Lord of Lords? The first thing to do is find a place and time for such an important conversation. Prayer must be planned. There is a sense in which prayer can be engaged in all day long. But time must also be put aside in order to visit with the King, and so plans should be made.

May I suggest that you take your calendar at the start of the week and pencil in time with the Lord every day? To see that appointment there in black and white sometimes helps you to keep it.

Finding a place can be more of a challenge. When I had young children, it was almost impossible to find a quiet spot. In desperation one day, I took the kids out of their playpen and climbed inside! This became a lifesaver for me, and in the busy days after I'd discovered this safe haven, the children learned to leave me alone. They decided that Mommy was a whole lot nicer when she got out than when she got in!

LEARN TO BE STILL

But I still haven't addressed the problem of what to do when you actually get everything in order and are ready to pray. For instance, what do you do about wandering thoughts?

Let me give you an illustration. We have a cute grandchild, Stephen, who learned at an early age to avoid his mother's eyes when she wanted to talk to him. This necessitated his mom catching up with him and capturing him in her arms. She then turned him around and, taking his little face in a firm grip, got down on his level. Then she said gently, "Look at me, Stephen!" Stephen's eyes rolled to the left, then to the right, then right up to the top of his head until only the whites could be seen! Judy kept at it, holding his little face until, slightly dizzy with all that eye rolling, Stephen finally focused his eyes on his mother's face, and then she could tell him what she wanted him to hear. The first thing she said was, "I love you, Stephen." Then she told him what she needed to tell him.

When you begin to pray, imagine that you are Stephen! Think about God, your heavenly Father, taking your face lovingly in His hands and holding you firmly right there in front of Him saying to you, "Look at me, Stephen." Stay still until you focus. In other words, be still and know that He is God (Ps. 46:10). When your thoughts are settled it's a good idea to start every time in God's presence with a period of silent prayer.

Try to form a habit of meeting with God without an agenda. So many of us have to teach or care for others that it is hard to come to God without thinking about them. Oh, we think, this Scripture would be excellent for Mrs. Smith. But God has things to say to us as well as to Mrs. Smith. We need to listen to God's voice without thinking of others and what would be good for them. First, God wants to tell us what is good for us. Listening to God is an important part of prayer. Try settling down to spend time quietly. Before you even begin to get down to the work of prayer, see if you can hear a thought, enjoy the stillness, or receive a new idea God wants you to think about.

In prayer, you have passive parts and active parts. Yet even the passive parts take work for some of us! It takes a huge effort to stop and be still, especially if we are active by nature. In the book of Hebrews, for example, the Lord says, "Make every effort to enter that rest" (Heb. 4:11). Here Paul puts two words together that do not appear to belong together at all, *effort* and *rest*. That sounds like another oxymoron. I am a very active person. It takes a big effort on my part to be quiet and still, but I must work at resting if I am to have any power in my prayer life. It is only after quieting our spirit that we will know what to pray and how to pray.

LOOK AT THOSE WHO PRAY WELL

There are many ways of learning about prayer. One way is to look at the lives of people who seem to have gotten a handle on it. Who prays prayers that work?

It is said that James, the brother of our Lord Jesus Christ, had a nickname that was given to him by the early church. He was called "camel knees"! The obvious inference is that James's knees resembled those of a camel because he was always kneeling! Hearing this caused me to wonder what my nickname might be!

We're going to take a close look at a prophet named Elijah. James pointed out that "Elijah was a man just like us. He prayed earnestly that it would not rain, and it did not rain on the land for three and a half years. Again he prayed, and the heavens gave rain, and the earth produced its crops" (Jas. 5: 17-18). Now there is a prayer that worked!

What sort of person do you need to be in order to be effective in your prayer life?

YOU HAVE TO LEARN TO BE PASSIONATE IN YOUR PRAYING

Elijah "prayed earnestly that it would not rain, and it did not rain" (Jas. 5:17). Elijah's heart was in his work. Many times we kneel to pray and we really don't care if God hears and answers us or not. Fervency is a condition of the heart that is developed through our growing relationship with God. As we grow to love Him, we find ourselves caring about the things He cares about. Prayer turns our thoughts away from our selfish concerns because we are putting ourselves into the presence of a selfless Being, and a little of that rubs off.

YOU NEED TO BE A PERSISTENT PRAY-ER IF YOU ARE TO SEE YOUR PRAYERS WORK

Elijah prayed continually about the work of God. He climbed a mountain and got to work. He set himself to watch and pray until the rain came (1 Kings 18:42-46). Most of us give up far too soon when we are praying. We hit an obstacle such as unanswered prayer and stop dead in our tracks. When Elijah set himself to pray on the top of Mount Carmel, you get the impression that he settled down until the answer came. God likes us to be persistent. Jesus told a story about a woman who persistently asked a judge to grant her request (Luke 18:1-8). And Jesus commended the persistent, blind beggar (Luke 18:35-43). He wants us to go on asking until it's the right time to get an answer. Persistence takes your prayer life into a whole new orbit. "Are any among you suffering? They should keep on praying about it," James tells us (Jas. 5:13).

PRAY WHEN TROUBLE TROUBLES YOU

There should be no excuse for any of us. It's not as if we have nothing to pray about! God has allowed enough trouble in all of our lives to keep us on our knees. And yet for some this could be the sticking point. It's hard to pray when trouble troubles us. Yet James sets his remarks about prayer in the context of trouble. "Is any one of you in trouble? He should pray," he says (Jas. 5:13). We should, but do we? It has been my experience that my prayer life seizes up as soon as trouble pokes its ugly head into my life.

16

But in the end I look back and recognize that without the trouble there would have been very little praying at all. If we are desperate enough, trouble forces us to spend time with God.

When we first came to live in America, our children were thrilled with the music programs in the public schools. All of them wanted to play an instrument. "I want to play the drums," seven-year-old Pete announced! I was aghast and hastily signed him up for clarinet! This was a serious mistake. The net result of all this was that he never practiced because he didn't want to play the clarinet; he wanted to play the drums. One day he came whistling into the room carrying his clarinet. "Pray for me, Mom," he said. "It's tryouts at school for band, and I want first chair clarinet!"

"I can't pray that for you, Pete. You haven't practiced in months."

"If I'd practiced, I wouldn't need you to pray," he retorted! Many of us are like Pete. We never practice prayer, but, when urgent business arises, we expect to know exactly what to say and how to say it. Trouble gives us the grand opportunity to practice for the concert.

What sort of trouble was James talking about? All sorts. Little troubles and big ones. He mentions relational troubles: "Confess your sins to each other" (Jas. 5:16); and he deals with sin troubles, "Whoever turns a sinner from the error of his way will save him from death and cover over a multitude of sins" (v. 20). Is any among you hurting? Has your spouse left you? Has someone mistreated you at work? Have you been

passed over or gotten the bad part of a deal?
Is there someone out there friendless, loveless,
childless, cashless, jobless, powerless, clueless?
Is anyone in trouble? He should pray!

Trouble is a great growth hormone. It takes us from
being spiritual dwarfs to spiritual giants—if we
respond rightly to it, that is. A few years ago, our
family moved into crisis mode. I listened to myself
praying. I was shocked. I heard myself pray like an
unbeliever. I was praying panic prayers, indulging
in angry tirades, and using bargaining language.
"Where is my prayer life just when I need it the
most?" I asked God. Hard on the heels of that thought
came the realization that this trouble was going to do
wonders for my prayer life! And it has. Trouble can, in
fact, jump-start our prayer life. If we respond to
divinely permitted trouble instead of reacting against
it, we will find that the situation does two things for us.
It will show us that our devotional life isn't working,
and it will show us how to work on making it work!

God is such a God of grace. Sometimes He must
feel very like the father whose son was in college and
who only got in touch when he wanted money! Does
the Lord hear from you and me only when we want
something? The amazing thing about the Lord is His
patient love. He will hear us out whenever we get
around to approaching Him.

So when trouble comes, don't resist it as if it is an
enemy; rather, welcome it as a friend. Let it drive you
to your knees. Think about it. If trials persist, it just
may be that you will persist in prayer. Looking back,
I can see how constant pressure kept me in the Lord's
presence, and for that I am grateful.

18

Never be afraid to ask God for the stars, but when God says no or wait, be willing to say, "Thy will be done," and ask the Lord for strength to live well in difficult circumstances. As we try to discover the secrets of prayer that works, it is my prayer that we will find our prayer life revolutionized.

2

Praying When Life Gets Hard

How can you talk to God when your heart is breaking?

by Nancy J. Nordenson

In a dimly lit hospital room, I stared out the window into the early morning darkness and waited for the drips of IV fluid to begin the contractions that would birth my lifeless midterm baby. My sorrow was lonely and deep. I wanted to pray, but there were no words to voice the thoughts that swirled in my mind.

When life is hard, prayer is hard. Grief, illness, depression, and anger invade our lives and hang on with tenacity, stealing our desire to pray and our belief in prayer just when we need them most. Physically and emotionally weary, we struggle to move from "Dear God" to "Amen." Simply getting through the day becomes our goal, leaving the luxury of connecting with God for better times.

I find it difficult to meet the expectations of Scripture regarding prayer. I fail to pray "with thanksgiving" (Phil. 4:6) when the situation I've prayed about for so long is only getting worse. How many of us pray "without ceasing" (1 Thess. 5:17, KJV) when waves of grief knock us over, pull us down, and hold us under? When disappointment and anger over dashed plans and failed relationships consume our thoughts and our unquiet hearts, where do we find the emotional energy to pray?

But God commands that we pray. He didn't make prayer optional; He doesn't hand us a signed excuse, releasing us from prayer, when life becomes difficult. God must have known that the process of thinking thoughts to an unseen "Something" might seem inadequate in the face of our own suffering, that spending time alone in our room, praying the same thing yet again, might seem better spent pacing. He must have known each of us would come to the difficult day when, faced with the urge or challenge to pray, we would instead say, "I just can't," and go no further.

In obedience to God's command, prayer must become what Oswald Chambers called "an effort of the will." When life is difficult, any effort can seem like too much. But if we explore ways of praying that may be easier with limited physical and emotional strength, we may more readily set our wills in the direction of prayer.

FIND A PRAYERFUL PLACE

Jesus often went to solitary places to pray, such as the mountaintop, the lake, and the garden (see Matt. 14:23, 26:36-46; Mark 1:35; and John 6:22-24). We can't always arrange a trip to a mountaintop, but we can find somewhere appealing to pray. Slip into a church sanctuary and look at the cross or stained-glass windows. Spend a quiet hour at a museum. Create a prayerful place in your home by lighting a candle or placing your chair by the window. Or simply go for a walk.

USE OTHERS' WORDS

When our prayers need words we can't seem to find, we can use someone else's. The Bible is filled with prayers. Consider the petitions of Moses as he struggled to lead God's people. Listen to the kings of Israel as they prayed for help in battle. Borrow the words of the psalmists as they prayed for deliverance, protection, and forgiveness. In the New Testament, meditate on the words of Jesus and the apostles.

For example, consider the prayer of King Jehoshaphat. A messenger greeted him with these words: "A vast army is coming against you" (2 Chron. 20:2). The future of his kingdom was in peril; he and his people were trapped by mighty opponents. The king listened to this message and then prayed: "We have no power to face this vast army that is attacking us. We do not know what to do, but our eyes are upon you" (v.12). I've borrowed these words of the besieged king when I've felt overpowered by circumstances outside of my control. His prayer is like a flare shot up to the God who rescues.

Consider using other written prayers as well, such as the words from hymns or from a book of prayers.

MEDITATE ON JESUS' LIFE

Jesus had a hard life. Can we find something in His life that mirrors our own difficult times? The gospels tell us about the time He prayed alone at night, so full of emotion that He sweat drops of blood. We can read about the betrayal by His friends and the religious establishment. We can wonder how He must have suffered over being misunderstood by His family.

Did He feel sorrow when He was rebuked rather than praised for performing a miracle? What was He thinking as He wept over His friend Lazarus' grave. How did He find the strength to put one foot in front of the other on the way to His own crucifixion? Can we relate to His cry on the cross, "My God, why have you forsaken me" (Matt. 27:46)?

Feeling scared and cowardly when I needed to be calm and brave, I thought about Jesus entering Jerusalem for the last time before His death. Even knowing what was ahead, Jesus walked right into His crisis. Horribly unfair things were about to happen to Him. Humiliation and death awaited. If He could walk into that, then with His strength, I could walk into the experience I was facing.

As we meditate upon Jesus' life in this way, we connect with Him and share our experience with Him. This, too, is a way of praying.

PRAY A REPEATED PHRASE

It can also be helpful to pray often using the same few words. These words can be prayed aloud, whispered, or said inwardly while engaged in another activity.

There is no magic in the repetition of these words. Rather, what you're seeking is a continual prayer, a constant reminder of the truth to which you so desperately need to cling, a focus for unfocused thoughts. The sudden onsets of panic and grief after the loss of my baby eased when I repeated Jesus' words over and over again: "Peace I leave with you; my peace I give to you" (John 14:27).

REMEMBER THE HOLY SPIRIT'S INTERCESSION

The advocacy of the Holy Spirit on our behalf is unceasing. Paul tells us that the Holy Spirit prays for us when we are weak, when we don't even know how to pray or what to pray for (see Rom. 8:26-27).

Just as a bewildered plaintiff or defendant—without ability to plead his own case before a judge and jury— asks an attorney to speak for him, so we can entrust our cause to the Holy Spirit and remain silent for a time. This silence does not imply a lack of interest in being before God but rather a choice to be represented by the petitions of the Holy Spirit.

ASSUME A POSTURE OF PRAYER

There is a good reason for the traditional prayer posture of closed hands and eyes: The less we see and touch, the more we focus on praying. But when our hearts and minds are racing, even this traditional prayer posture can be inadequate to help us focus. Sometimes, we may need a more intentional posture, such as kneeling or even lying prostrate on the floor. With our faces to the floor, we find ourselves in the company of others who have cried out to God from this position: Ezekiel, in despair; Ezra, ashamed and disgraced; Daniel, terrified; Jesus, sorrowful and troubled.

WRITE IT ONCE

Simply thinking about our problems before praying may emotionally exhaust or dredge up resentment or anger. When I described to a friend my struggle to pray about a difficult situation, she advised me to write out a prayer that covered all the aspects of the problem. Then she suggested I read this prayer whenever I felt the need to pray, focusing my heart and mind on the words I'd already written. What a relief it was to have a plan for prayer, so I wouldn't need to search the pain daily, starting from scratch.

SHOW, DON'T TELL

When Sennacherib sent a letter to King Hezekiah threatening to destroy Jerusalem, Hezekiah read it and immediately went to the temple. He spread the letter out before the Lord and began to pray (see 2 Kings 19).

Could our prayers be supported by a visual aid as well? By using images rather than words, we can bypass the energy needed to find the words. With one action we can lay our situation before the God who sees as well as hears. Spread the stack of bills, the antidepressant prescription, or the abnormal biopsy report before Him. Tell God by showing God.

PRAY WITH YOUR TEARS

Mary wept at Jesus' feet after the death of her brother, Lazarus (see John 11:32-33). Can you recall a time when you cried with another person? Do you remember the emotional release and subsequent bonding with that person after the tears? We can open our hearts to God and deepen our relationship with Him by crying in His presence, offering our tears as prayers.

EXPRESS YOUR ANGER

Anger blocks communication. Are you angry at God over your situation? If so, tell Him how you feel. Follow Job's example of talking to God with honesty and respect. Talk it out, write it down, and watch for His answer.

BE SILENT

Only the best of friends can sit together silently with ease. The psalmist reminds us to "be still, and know that I am God" (Ps. 46:10) and reassures us that "the LORD Almighty is with us" (v. 11). Allow yourself to sit silently in the presence of God.

ASK OTHERS TO PRAY

To release God's power on the battlefield below, Moses' friends helped him hold up his staff (see Ex. 17:8-13). In the same way, the prayers of others support us and release the power of God into the battles of our lives. If you don't know of at least one person who is committed to praying for you, ask someone.

As I stared out the window in that hospital room, I had a definite sense of others praying for me. My loneliness eased and the struggle to pray relaxed. I didn't have to search for the words anymore; I knew the words of someone else would bring me before God.

DO YOU BELIEVE?

At the memorial service we held for our infant daughter, we read the words spoken by Jesus to a grieving Martha four days after the death of her brother. Jesus said to her: "I am the resurrection and the life.... Do you believe this?" Martha replied, "Yes, Lord"

(John 11:25-27). Jesus then proceeded to the tomb, twice overcome with emotion before arriving. Moments later Lazarus walked out of the tomb, resurrected.

Despair and belief, sorrow and joy, death and life, waiting and rescue are the threads woven together in the fabric of this story. They are also the fabric of my story and perhaps yours. As with Martha, our hope when life gets hard rests in the way we answer Jesus' question: "I am the resurrection and the life. Do you believe this?" If we can say yes, no matter how we choose to pray about the difficulties we face, we know that we leave our prayers in trustworthy hands.

Reprinted from Discipleship Journal, *issue 116. Used with permission.*

3

Why Won't I Pray with My Wife?

Breaking barriers to spiritual intimacy.

by Dr. Louis McBurney

A sick feeling takes over the pit of my stomach. The pastor's wife I'm counseling has just brought up a topic I'd rather avoid. Nancy is registering her hurt at the hands of her pastor husband—and nailing me in the process.

"I remember how excited I was when we fell in love, and I realized I was going to be married to a minister," she says. "I had always prayed for a godly husband, a man who would be a spiritual leader for me and our children. I was sure Joe would be God's answer to those prayers. We even prayed together on our dates. It gave me such a secure feeling.

"I just don't know what happened. After we got married all of that stopped. Oh, sometimes we still pray together or read the Bible, but only if I insist. That doesn't feel right. I want him to take the leadership for our spiritual life together."

I'm gulping hard and nodding knowingly—too knowingly. I've heard my wife echo similar concerns. One of my frequent failures: not taking initiative for spiritual closeness in marriage.

Why is spiritual intimacy with my wife so easy to avoid?

REASONABLE EXCUSES

I've discovered I'm not alone. Most of the ministers we counsel at Marble Retreat also struggle with this problem. Some common explanations have emerged.

The first is the professional exhaustion defense. It goes something like this: "I have to keep up this mask of religiosity almost all the time. From morning till night I'm the minister. I can't just be me. I'm always the one called on to pray everywhere I go. The only other guy who's prayed at Kiwanis in the past four years is Father O'Roarke. Men in the locker room at the health club apologize for cussing in front of me. I'm always expected to have scriptural answers for every question and deliver them with a loving smile.

"I get sick of it. Home is the only place I can relax and be real. I want to share spiritual things with my wife, but quite frankly, when she says, 'Can't we pray together?' I feel attacked. Then I feel guilty. Then I feel angry. Then I just want to escape."

I can't use this excuse, however; I'm a shrink, not a man of the cloth.

However, the second one, the hypocrisy factor, does fit. My wife, Melissa, sees me offering sound spiritual counsel to others, but she knows I'm no saint. Sometimes I'm reluctant to pray with my wife because of this rationale:

"Melissa knows the real me. It's fine to offer holy solutions and wise biblical advice to others, but I can't get away with that at home. She knows I'm not very disciplined. She's seen my temper. She puts up with my pouts."

"She remembers the ways I've hurt her through the years by my selfishness or lust or thoughtless actions. She knows what I've been like as a father to our children. I'd feel like a total hypocrite expounding some Scripture to her or offering some pious prayer. She'd crucify me."

"No, it's safer to just play the game. She knows me too well. Maybe someday when I get my act together…"

Of course, the problem with that is I'll never get my act together. I need at least one place I can let down and be real. That seems more necessary than devotions.

The third factor is the spiritual dwarf syndrome. Many ministers believe, often accurately, that their spouse is a spiritual giant compared to themselves. They feel dwarfed by her deep faith. She doesn't seem to agonize with the same gut-wrenching doubts and questions as he.

Her quietly committed prayer life shines compared to his hasty, often desperate prayers fired off on the run. The Word seems to speak to her. Ages have passed since he has even read the Scriptures to find God's message for himself, and she wants him to be her "spiritual leader"?

How can he risk the vulnerability that spiritual union would bring? She'd find out how shallow he really is. He feels less dwarfish behind the pulpit. Better stay there. It's definitely safer.

HOLY DISHARMONY

Another obstacle to spiritual intimacy is holy disharmony. Distinctive belief differences or style preferences may create dissonance when you try to pray, worship, or interpret Scripture together. Rather than unifying, it divides. You both agree with Paul that your joy would be complete if you were only of one mind, but that's about all you agree on. Common areas of disagreement include preference for time of day, interpretation of Scripture, devotional style, and issues of trust.

Melissa is a morning person, for example. For her, the most meaningful devotional experiences are flooded by the first rays of the rising sun. I'm pretty convinced, however, that God doesn't wake up till mid afternoon. I'm sure the splendor of starlight was created to bathe our expressions of worship. That difference seems trivial until we try to adjust our biological clocks to find time for devotional togetherness.

If your devotional time together includes reading Scripture, you may find tension in how you interpret what you read. One of you may thoroughly enjoy lively debate, discussing various interpretations. The other may shrink from such encounters, preferring to find a practical application or an inspiring devotional thought. It is easy for a win/lose dynamic to emerge that quickly poisons the wellspring of shared spirituality.

Another difference is style. When praying together, this includes the volume of words, the use of the language of Zion versus the vernacular, who does the praying, what resources are chosen, and what physical posture is preferred. If our mate's style is too divergent from our own, the feeling of genuine contact with God may be destroyed.

A friend of mine told me once that he couldn't pray with his wife. By the time they finished, he felt his prayer had been rated like an Olympic diver. He usually got only about a 6.0. His wife went on to a 9.5 performance.

DIGGING OUT

So what's to be done? Most clergy couples agree they need the sense of spiritual oneness. Wives particularly crave the feeling of closeness nurtured in those moments of bondedness before the Lord. Avoidance or a frustrated acceptance of failure doesn't bring much peace.

You don't have to remain stuck, though, in the ditch of spiritual estrangement. Here are some steps Melissa and I have found helpful for others and ourselves.

1. Identify the problem.

Clear an afternoon or evening in your schedule to discuss this area of your relationship. Allow no interruptions, and covenant together to make understanding (not agreement) your goal. Enter the time without your usual agenda of proving who's right and who's wrong. Believe me, you both are—right and wrong.

Trace the history of your spiritual relationship, recalling the times it went well and the times it didn't work for you. Then try to identify how you've felt inside about having a time of spiritual conversation.

Try not to let "time demands" be the rationalization. As difficult as it is, I find most people make time for the things that reward them. Push beyond your busy schedules, and search for deeper problems.

Your goal is to understand each other in a nonjudgmental way. You may be uncomfortable with how your mate feels, but accept her perception as the truth from which she acts.

2. Clarify expectations.

I used to believe Melissa wanted me to be something I'm not. She would talk about her desire for me to be more of a spiritual leader for her. That sounded pretty overwhelming to me. So rather than risk embarrassment or failure, I'd avoid even trying. I interpreted her expectations as wanting me to lead in deep discussion of the Scriptures or to expound on some dramatic vision the Lord had given me (a fresh one for each day, of course).

When I finally told her what I thought she craved, she was flabbergasted. I'll never forget the relief I felt when she said, "Oh, that's not what I want. I just want a spiritual companion, not a leader."

Often our expectations are totally unrealistic or simply indescribably vague. We may have developed an image of what spiritual sharing is supposed to look like from some conference or a book we read, but never stopped to define it clearly with our mate.

3. Renegotiate a contract.

When I had a clearer idea of Melissa's expectations, I felt more comfortable working toward an agreement.

What would "spiritual companionship" look like to her? What were specific things I could do that would invite her into my soul life?

As it turned out, what she'd been wanting was much easier than what I'd been assuming. We began to spend a short time at breakfast reading Scripture (usually a paragraph or maybe a chapter), and then praying together briefly about our individual concerns. It also helps when I talk about how the Lord is working in my heart. At times we get together for a longer period of prayer or discussion, usually when life's pressures seem to be closing in.

4. Avoid criticism.

You can be pretty sure that you're going to blow it somewhere along the way. You'll get busy or be angry with each other, or somebody will have the flu, and then you won't do it the way you intended. When that happens, refuse to place blame and judgment anywhere. That's deadly.

5. Celebrate your steps toward spiritual oneness.

Every time Melissa tells me how good she feels when I initiate sharing, I get a renewed commitment to the process. Our unity is reinforced each time we tell others about the importance of having a soul mate as our spouse—for example, when we're with friends and I tell them that Melissa and I were praying together for them the other day, or when she says, "Louis and I were just reading that Scripture recently."

Those comments are ways we let each other know how satisfying our spiritual closeness is.

Ours has been a rocky pilgrimage in this area. But we're finding a new sense of freedom and safety. Our growing spiritual oneness is helping us enjoy more fully the other dimensions of our lives together, whether long walks hand in hand or our sexual intimacy. It's still not easy, but the strength and joy we experience together makes the struggle worthwhile.

4

Praying Below the Surface

It's okay to pray for our spiritual needs.

by Pamela S. Binkley

As I prayed I knew something was missing. Requests from the women in my Bible study group had grown predictable. Concerns about health, careers, cantankerous cars, financial needs, and trying relationships packed my prayer journal. I'd even prayed about two leaky roofs.

Shouldn't there be requests for spiritual needs?
I wondered. Not that the prayers in my journal were insignificant. Along with the other women, I'd learned by His answers that God's love for us and the ingenuity of His solutions to our problems defy the imagination. He tends to our daily needs even as He tends to our souls. Besides, one of those leaky roofs was mine!

But were there other prayers God wanted me to offer up for these women? The answer surfaced the year our leader challenged us: "As you study the letters of Paul, look for the prayers he prayed for the churches and pray each one for your group."

My first discovery occurred in 1 Thessalonians 5:23, a petition for purity. I knelt and asked, "May the spirit, soul, and body of each woman be kept blameless at the coming of our Lord Jesus Christ." Surely, this prayer was holy to God. I began to understand that God wants us to pray for daily needs, but He also wants us to pray for our spiritual needs.

Here are some of the prayers I found as I continued scouting Paul's epistles. Pray them for your small group, your Sunday school class, your friends, or your family. Put them in your own words. Identify what keeps us from enjoying these spiritual qualities and ask God to remove those hindrances.

A PRAYER FOR FILLING AND SPILLING

"May the God of hope fill you with all joy and peace as you trust in Him so that you may overflow with hope by the power of the Holy Spirit" (Rom.15:13).

I pray that the women in my group will know this kind of trust in God, and will act on His promises. One woman did just that when she felt vulnerable to a temptation. A man she knew kept calling her when her husband was out of town. She asked God to remove the temptation those phone calls represented, based on His promise not to tempt us beyond what we are able to withstand. The next time her husband went out of town, she discovered she could make outgoing calls, but couldn't receive incoming ones. God kept her tempter from calling at a time when she felt weak.

What are the enemies of trust? Pessimism, fearfulness, and timidity all threaten our ability to trust God. So I pray for confidence and courage. What keeps your group or family from trusting God?

A PRAYER FOR UNITY

"May the God who gives endurance and encouragement give you a spirit of unity among yourselves as you follow Christ Jesus, so that with one heart and mouth you may glorify the God and Father of our Lord Jesus Christ" (Rom. 15:5-6).

The first night our study group meets in September, I listen to the women introduce themselves and wonder how such a diverse group will bond. They are CPAs, crossing guards, mothers, teachers, physicians, and office workers. Some work 50-hour weeks; some are retired. They represent different races, marital statuses, incomes, and denominations. One or two may be unchurched. Several talk at the same time. Another sits without saying a word. As I pray Paul's prayer for unity, I ask God to keep our differences from pulling us apart. I pray He'll turn our diversity into zest for getting to know one another. I ask that our focus would be on Him, not ourselves.

It never fails; at some point during the year I look around and see how God has taken all our differences and arranged them in a perfect bouquet. Our dissimilarities blend because we are following Christ. He makes us one with Him and with each other.

A PRAYER TO KNOW GOD BETTER

"I keep asking that the God of our Lord Jesus Christ, the glorious Father, may give you the Spirit of wisdom and revelation so that you may know Him better. I pray also that the eyes of your heart may be enlightened in order that you may know the hope to which He has called you, the riches of His glorious inheritance in the saints, and His incomparably great power for us who believe" (Eph. 1:17-19).

With this prayer as my model, I ask God to free the women in my group from the cobwebs in their thinking. Sometimes the cobwebs are beliefs that God can hardly wait for us to fail so He can punish us. When that's the case, I pray for His love to become a reality. Sometimes the cobwebs are a lack of strength to do the things we want to do. Then I pray for God's power to become real. Years ago, this empowerment enabled me to quit smoking.

In our discussions I listen for words like, "I used to think..." That's my clue that someone is about to clear out a cobweb and share a newly learned truth.

Key to knowing God is a commitment to read and study Scripture. I pray that each woman will seek out that private place and block of time God has given her. I ask that her time with God would be so rich she will refuse to let the pressures of the day grab it away from her.

I also pray that as each woman becomes familiar with Scripture she will not stop learning about God—that none of us will ever settle back with an I-have-arrived attitude. As we continue to see how great God is, we must surely see how minuscule our godliness and our knowledge is in comparison.

A PRAYER FOR SALT-AND-LIGHT LOVE

"And this is my prayer: that your love may abound more and more in knowledge and depth of insight, so that you may be able to discern what is best and may be pure and blameless until the day of Christ, filled with the fruit of righteousness that comes through Jesus Christ—to the glory and praise of God" (Phil. 1:9-11).

I ask God to instill in our group of women a love for others like Christ's love for us. This love is more than a pat on the back and a smile for one who is deeply distressed. Rather it is a love that sits down and listens. It is a love that empathizes and encourages, it's a salt-and-light love that speaks what is true. When it offers advice, that counsel comes from a storage bin of Christ's wisdom.

Such love points others toward Christ instead of trying to garner glory for itself. It is a love that sometimes surprises, because it loves even those who are not so easy to love. Pray that your group will see others with the eyes of Christ. Pray that their love will be fruitful because it points others toward God. Pray they will love even when the object of their love doesn't deserve it, acknowledging that Christ's love, too, is undeserved.

A PRAYER FOR SHARING FAITH

"I pray that you may be active in sharing your faith, so that you will have a full understanding of every good thing we have in Christ" (Phil. 6).

We share our faith by telling and doing. I pray that the women in my group will share their faith in both these ways, and that as they do; their faith will become more real to them.

I also pray that we will tell others about our faith. Timidity often hinders us from sharing, so I pray for the courage to speak out. Caring about what others think is another hindrance to witnessing, so I pray we will not be influenced by what people think of us.

MORE THAN MEETS THE EYE

The answers to prayers like these are not as tangible as the answers to prayers about cantankerous cars and leaky roofs. Sometimes the answers are long in coming. Spiritual qualities, like oak trees, take time to mature. Sometimes the answers are hidden from us because they represent private victories. If you become discouraged because you don't see the results of your spiritual petitions, ask God to let you see just enough so that you will persevere.

When I'm inclined to lose heart in prayer, I picture the Old Testament high priests. They entered the Holy of Holies, bearing the names of the 12 tribes of Israel carved on stones and worked into the breastplate. Because of Jesus, each of us is now a priest. We, too, can enter the Holy of Holies, carrying the names of those we pray for, and equipped with model prayers from Paul.

5

When God Says No

Accepting God's will
when it clashes with your own.

by Sheila S. Hudson

The smell of antiseptics mingled with those of perfume and coffee as thirty of us wedged into the St. Mary's Hospital waiting room. We patiently sat, crumpled tissues in hand, occasionally punctuating the awkward silence with conversation.

Tears and smiles traded places on my face, while a fist of fear grew ever larger in my stomach: The doctor called the family into a private room. We joined hands and prayed. For me, this scene was too familiar. How would I react this time? How would my faith respond to the challenge if God answered my prayer for Becky's recovery with "no"?

At dinner the waitress asked if we wanted anything else. Tim, my husband, began to softly weep. He looked away. I explained to her that we had just lost a loved one. She gave a compassionate nod and retreated. "Go ahead and cry," I said squeezing his hand, "for tomorrow at the funeral, you'll need to comfort Shawn."

This was the fourth close friend I have recently lost. Barbara died of complications following childbirth. Sheila struggled and finally succumbed to cancer. Jean lost her battle with congestive heart failure. Becky, a young wife and mother, died suddenly of a cerebral aneurysm.

Each time that my prayers seemed futile, I asked God, "Why?" Death could have stalked someone less kind or worthy. Why was Becky, a wife, mother, accomplished musician, and teacher, snatched away with only a headache for a warning? Why did Barbara's child die? Why did she follow her infant daughter a few months later? Why did Shelia suffer with cancer and Jean struggle to breathe with congestive heart failure? Why did God choose to take them and not heal them? Why did God say "no"?

Prayer is a living thing. It is a two-way conversation with God. And God, our heavenly Father, has many responses. One of these is "no." As mature Christians, we must be able to accept the answers that God gives, realizing it will not always be the answer that we want. God has better plans. His ways are not our ways and His thoughts are not our thoughts (see Isa. 55:8-9). The understanding of what God is doing in our lives may not come until years later, if at all.

The Apostle Paul struggled with a "thorn in the flesh." He constantly prayed for it to be removed, but God said "no." Moses had a speaking problem, but God didn't remove it. Instead He sent him a sidekick. Jesus asked for the "cup" to be removed the night before His crucifixion, but God said "no" and enabled Him to bear the cross. Why should we think we are somehow exempt from tragedy and pain?

44

Many Christians have not taken the time or made the effort to develop a healthy, vibrant prayer life. They find themselves much like John Donne who stated, "I throw myself down in my chamber, and I call in, and invite God, and His Angels thither, and when they are there, I neglect God and His Angels, for the noise of a fly, for the rattling of a coach, for the whining of a door."

Prayer requires work and persistence, but the rewards of a richer walk with God are worth the effort. Pursuing God in prayer will develop a deeper faith and shatter the concept that God is unconcerned about our personal struggles. A deeper faith will enable us to accept God's answers, even the times when He says "no" to our most heartfelt requests.

My faith says that God will raise up another to teach the beginners. My hope says the Holy Spirit will convict another to cook and serve meals in Christ's name. My love says Jesus will plant the desire in another musician to accompany the choir. God's agenda *will* be accomplished. He still needs music to be played, finger-paint artists to be encouraged, choirs to sing, and cookies—especially chocolate chip—to be baked.

The fragrance of the carnations and lilies brings my mind back to the gravesite. We clasp hands with those of our Christian family and commit our sister to heaven. Though God replied "no" to our request for Becky's healing, He said "yes" to resurrection and her eternal life in heaven with Him! This thought inspires me to look to the future with hope no matter what answers to prayer I receive!

6

Running Out of Prayers

**Hardships can often lead us
to new ways of praying.**

by Jill Briscoe

Have you ever run out of prayers? I'm sure you have. Was it after failure or success? We can understand our prayer life being affected when we are in trouble, but what about it being affected by achievement?

After Elijah ran to Jezreel, toward victory and acclamation, God vindicated him by fire. But suddenly Elijah turned and ran in the opposite direction.

When Ahab got home, he told Jezebel that Elijah had slaughtered the prophets of Baal. So Jezebel sent this message to Elijah: "May the gods also kill me if by this time tomorrow I have failed to take your life like those whom you killed."

Elijah was afraid and fled for his life. He went to Beersheba, and on alone into the desert. He sat down under a solitary broom tree and prayed that he might die. "I have had enough, Lord," he said. "Take my life, for I am no better than my ancestors" (1 Kings 19:1-4.

Elijah ran away from Jezreel and into the jaws of defeat. He was just like us, human and afraid. Yes, he was afraid! (1 Kings 19:3. This particular verse of Scripture is an amazing verse. I could imagine the Bible saying that Elijah was exhausted or angry or lonely, but not "Elijah was afraid!" Yet, that particular verse of Scripture encourages me to keep hoping, because I, too, am often afraid.

What happens when we run out of faith and run into fear? Do we end up like Elijah, flat on our faces under the proverbial broom tree? (v. 4. It has been my experience that when you run into fear you can run out of faith in a hurry. Fear paralyzes you. I have always been a fearful person. When I was a child, I feared I wouldn't ever grow up. When I did grow up, I feared I would never live long enough to get married. When I got married, I was frightened I would never have children. When I had three, I worried that they would never get married and have children. And so on and so forth.

I am very familiar with the fear that chases faith away. And it can all happen in a moment! It might feel final, as I'm sure it did to Elijah, but as we shall see, this fear would lead to a whole new dimension of ministry and experience in prayer.

WHAT FEAR DOES TO FAITH

Stuart and I live in Wisconsin, where snow and ice are a big part of our lives during the long winter months. Sometimes we get a blizzard. You can be inching along, and all of a sudden you run into what is called a "whiteout." You literally go blind for a moment and become disoriented as the snow swirls around the windshield.

We can experience whiteouts in our faith life too. We could call these experiences whiteouts, or "doubt outs."

You see perfectly clearly one moment, and the next you are blinded by the storm. Doubt is faith in distress, and it is very hard to pray when you are doubting God. The Bible says, "Anyone who wants to come to Him must believe that there is a God and that He rewards those who sincerely seek Him" (Heb. 11:6. Elijah was experiencing a mammoth "doubt out." He couldn't see God anymore, but he could see Jezebel. And she looked so much bigger than God.

It's funny what things people are afraid of, isn't it? Here is Elijah, who has taken on an entire nation, running away from a woman! But then, doubt and exhaustion do strange things to you. It's easy to lose perspective.

WHAT GOD'S PRESENCE DOES FOR US

The first thing to do when you arrive under the broom tree is to quit everything. Elijah didn't pretend. He simply said, "God, I've had it!" Elijah was experiencing serious burnout. Be encouraged to be this honest when your turn comes. God wants us to say whatever we want to say.

If we are talking about intercession, we must believe that God is a rewarder of "those who sincerely seek Him." When you're under the broom tree, your prayers are not intercessory prayers but rather prayers of desperation. Yet Hallesby encourages us to pray on, even when we are driving through a blizzard of unbelief! He says:

Many have had most remarkable answers to prayer when they had no clear or definite assurance that they would be heard. It has seemed to them that God has given the most remarkable answers to prayer at times when they had no faith whatsoever!

Keep talking to the Lord even if you are mad at Him or doubting His very existence. Jesus promised that a sparrow would never fall without the Father knowing it. Note, He never promised that a sparrow would not fall, but He did promise the sparrow would not fall without the Father's knowledge of it. God is never surprised by our visits to the broom tree.

Let's see what happened to the humbled prophet under his trauma tree.

GOD DEALS WITH OUR DISAPPOINTMENT

I find that when I'm checking into the Broom Tree Inn, I lose my perspective of God. All I can think about is how disappointed God must be with me. I become convinced that He is telling me to get my act together and share the Four Spiritual Laws with Jezebel!

I have to remind myself that I can never surprise God. In fact, all that God expects from us is failure of one kind or another along our spiritual road. The good news is; He waits around the corner of our failure. He has a plan—a plan of renewal and refreshment— and He waits at the reception desk of Broom Tree Inn, ready and eager to check us in! What we need to do is

cooperate. We should lie down and sleep again
(1 Kings 19:5-7.

Whatever medicine God the Healer prescribes;
we should take it. And we should rest long enough for
the loving treatment to take effect. Elijah waited until
he was strong enough to go on before he went on.

What brought you to this point? Was it a church that
hurt you or a spouse who abandoned you? Maybe
you are under the broom tree because of things you
cannot change. Perhaps you are the victim of a cruel
circumstance. Wrong choices that others made have
had severe consequences for you. Perhaps, like Elijah,
you are mostly disappointed with yourself. It is only
a matter of time before you decide that God can do
without you and so can everyone else!

I can remember getting into that state of mind only
once. My husband was out of town and my father was
sick. Things were not going well in the youth work I
was responsible for, and then our daughter broke her
arm. Stuart was in America making plans for us to
immigrate and I was supposed to be wrapping up our
work and packing up the house.

One day I couldn't ignore the gnawing pain in my
stomach anymore, so I went to the doctor. He told me
I was suffering from an ulcer, and he put me in the
hospital. Suffering from a great imagination as well as
a bleeding ulcer, I was quite sure that I was going to
die and that this would be a lot better for all concerned.
God would give Stuart an American wife who could
do the job in the states a whole lot better than I could,
and everyone would benefit.

As I think back to how the Lord lifted me out of my deep despondency, I realize that God may have allowed me to go through it so I could encourage others. Looking back, I can see that my experience was not unlike Elijah's.

The first thing both of us received was physical help. If you are in this predicament, have yourself checked out. It isn't unspiritual to look after your body. People helped me practically, and I had to learn to let them. God brought Elijah breakfast; friends brought my family supper!

And then I found lots of help in the Word about God's great concern for me. "The journey is too great for you," I read over and over again. God was not mad at me for being in the state I was in; He was loving and caring and infinitely patient. Above all, I became convinced that God was not finished with me yet. Failure is never final.

God "touched" His servant Elijah at the lowest point of his life, and God touched me as well. I continued on my way, strengthened by the nourishment He provided through the Bible, Christian friends, and above all, prayer. God will find a way to touch you if you give Him a chance to minister grace to you.

WHAT THE BROOM TREE GIVES TO US

The broom tree experiences in our lives introduce us to a new way of praying. It's not verbal praying but rather a total abandonment of ourselves in despair at God's feet. It is a wordless praying, a silent scream for help. Sometimes we cannot even shout at God. We are spent.

When you run out of prayers, God can still hear you! Even though no words are formed or spoken, God looks at you and reads the language of your longing. At that moment, you see, you are the prayer! So be content to just be a desperate prayer under your particular broom tree, and wait and see what happens!

You may wonder how long you will be there. You'll remain there as long as it takes for you to be strengthened. Try not to take on anything extra until things begin to be resolved. Once Elijah was off and running again, God went ahead of him, preparing his future. That is definitely what happened to me.

Stuart said that I had to stay put in England until I was well enough to face the immigration process, and I gradually regained my health and began to pack for the journey to the states. God went ahead of me every step of the way.

How will you know God has touched you and that it is time to move on? You will know if you sense God's love and acceptance. You will feel this sense of inner well-being far deeper than at the emotional level. The Holy Spirit does not come into our hearts to do His deepest work in the shallowest part of us. He works His healing grace at the mind level first. Once you hear Him saying something kind and sweet, believe it, get up from under your broom tree and go on to Horeb, the mountain of God.

If Elijah had not believed that "God was not finished with him yet," he would have died of a broken heart under the broom tree. If I had not believed that I was redeemable, I would have tried to persuade my husband to stay home and not immigrate to America. As I lay miserably alone in that hospital bed, I remember giving a desperate glance heavenward. It was all I could manage, but it was enough. *I am a prayer, Lord*, I said without words. *Read me*. Words are nice, but words are not needed when you are under the broom tree. Just be content to know that every word you would have said, if you could have said it, is heard loud and clear among the angels and by the Lord. His ears are especially tuned to those sorts of prayers—to the solitary, silent scream!

So where does this leave our hero? Sadder and wiser, certainly. Elijah came to terms with his fallen humanity. The expert on the subject of prayer learned that there are some times when you run out. You run out of faith, out of energy, out of friends, and out of hope. You run out of the human resources to function anymore. You run out of belief, and you run out of ideas, and you even run out of prayers. When that happens, God has only just begun! As Elijah was to find out, God gives more grace, more help, more joy, more hope, and more strength to all of us in our weakness than He ever does when we are strong. We just need to bank on it.

7

On the Wings of a Stranger's Prayers

Carrying one another's burdens in prayer.

by Shelly Esser

A number of years ago I went through a very dark period in my life—one of those dark night of the soul experiences. Having always processed difficulties through writing, I sat down at the computer and wrote a very candid article about my struggles. Thinking it might help someone else; I sent it off to be published. To my surprise, it was.

In the weeks that followed, I was inundated with letters and phone calls from all over the country. One of those letters came from an elderly nun named Sister George Towle. She wrote me a heartfelt letter expressing her commitment to pray for me daily. I was touched, but unbelievingly tossed the letter aside. She and many others had said, "I'll pray for you." I often wondered how many of those people actually kept their promise. Too often it seems we use that phrase so casually that it just becomes mere words of comfort. How many would not only dare pray for someone they don't know, but do so daily?

One day while collecting the mail, some five years later, I was astonished to discover another letter from Sister George Towle.

My dear Shelly,
   I am just taking a chance in God's providence and love for us that you will get this letter. Remember back in 1995, I wrote to you after reading your article.
I wanted you to know that I have prayed for you every day of my life!
   And I have often wondered how you are and what has happened to you, and lately the inspiration to write and ask you has become so strong that I felt it God urging me to write to you.
My heart, prayers, and love still go out to you,
Sister George

God had put it on a stranger's heart, for reasons I don't understand, to pray for me. Looking back, there is no doubt that one of the reasons I made it through those difficult years was because I was carried on the wings of a stranger's prayers.

Sister George and I continued to correspond until her death at age 90 two summers ago. She was one of the greatest sources of encouragement and prayer support that I have ever known, and I felt a great loss when she died, feeling like I had lost my most powerful prayer warrior.

This whole experience has gotten me thinking about how many people out there are dependent on our prayers. We have no idea what the people God may be putting on our hearts are going through and how our prayers may be His vehicle to carry them through.

There were months when the only prayers I could pray were deep groans and sobs. How comforting to know God had enlisted a stranger to fill those gaps and pray for me in ways I couldn't myself. Not only has this experience changed my view about prayer, it's enlarged my view of God.

To think that God loves us so much that He will put us on the heart of someone we don't even know to carry us in prayer for years is just a small example of how personal God is. God's gesture of having Sister George pray for me showed His amazing love for me in my brokenness. I'm thankful for that kind of God, and I'm thankful for the kind of servant who obediently followed through when God laid a stranger on her heart. Even in the dark places of our lives, God manages to reveal Himself in the most unexpected ways to remind us that we are never forgotten, no matter how dark it feels.

When Jesus, the greatest intercessor, taught His disciples how to pray, He not only instructed them on how to pray for themselves, but how to reach out and pray for others as well. Intercessory prayer is simply seeking the presence and audience of God for another. We are to carry one another's burdens as Galatians 6:2 says. Interceding for one another is one of the most valuable things we can do for each other.

Scripture admonishes us to pray, and much of this praying we are to do is for strangers. 1 Timothy 2:1 says, "I urge, then, first of all, that requests, prayers, intercession and thanksgiving be made for everyone..." We're to pray for those in authority, the lost, the brokenhearted, the poor, etc. How much of my praying is for the stranger? God places people along the paths of our lives for a purpose. Many times that purpose is to intercede on their behalf.

We may be the only person praying for them, but do we? How regularly are we really standing in the gap for others, particularly those we don't know? I wonder where I'd be today if Sister George hadn't held me up in prayer daily through the darkest night of my soul.

The kind of intercession that Sister George engaged in for me, and that you and I are called to, is a laying down of our lives for others. It is a sacrificing of our time for those in need. It is essentially a ministry of outreach.

It means we follow through when we promise to pray for someone. John Calvin said, "To make intercession for men is the most powerful and practical way in which we can express our love for them." God chose to have a stranger love me through intercession, and it changed my life. Who needs to be carried on the wings of your prayers?

8

Not My Will, But Yours

How to pray like Jesus.

by Michelle Lazurek

I have a confession to make: I don't know how to pray.

I've prayed my entire life, but I don't pray the way God wants me to pray, or even as His example demonstrates.

God revealed this to me while I was driving to a conference last year. God did not speak harshly to me, but in His gentle way convicted my heart in a way only His Spirit can do.

God gently asked me, "Why don't you come to Me when you want things?" Immediately, my heart ached. In response, I started to cry. Then He gave me a vision of my hand and, when I opened my hand, I saw a stone.

I had always *thought* I came to God in prayer and asked God for what I wanted, but in that moment, I realized I came to God, but I didn't *expect* Him to grant the desires of my heart. In fact, I came to Him much like small children running to their parents, expecting them to become a genie in a bottle to grant my every desire. But when He says no, I pump my fist in the air and I kick the sand and I don't want to talk to Him anymore. I feel defeated—what would be the purpose of speaking to Him if He's not going to give me what I asked, right?

Wrong!

I came to God much like Luke describes in chapter 11:11-13: "Which of you fathers, if your son asks for a fish, will give him a snake instead? Or if he asks for an egg, will give him a scorpion? If you then, though you are evil, know how to give good gifts to your children, how much more will your Father in heaven give the Holy Spirit to those who ask him!"

I would ask Him for what I wanted—my desires— some were selfish, others were selfless. I did the obligatory prayer for friends, relatives, etc. But in the back of my mind, I doubted. I didn't expect God to move miraculously in my life. I'm not even sure I even expected Him to answer the request positively. For me, the Christian life has not been easy. The road to becoming a disciple has been a rocky one. I've had a lot of disappointments that have calloused my heart against coming to God in boldness. *My lack of prayer has even affected my level of faith.*

God is the author of our prayers. He knows everything we will pray from now until the day we die. He put the desires of our hearts within us so we can ask Him and increase our faith. The purpose of our prayers is not for God; its purpose is to change us.

Maybe you can relate to my prayer struggles. Maybe you, like me, have kicked sand and ignored God after you didn't get what you wanted. If I can increase my prayer life, and ultimately my faith, then so can you.

Here are three ways for you to pray God-sized prayers:

PRAY WITH EXPECTATION

Matthew 7:8-11 says, "Which of you, if your son asks for bread, will give him a stone? Or if he asks for a fish, will give him a snake? If you, then, though you are evil, know how to give good gifts to your children, how much more will your Father in heaven give good gifts to those who ask him!"

Oftentimes I pray for what I want, but not what I need. God always gives us what we need, whether or not we even know we need it.

When the disciples asked Jesus how to pray, He replied with this: Luke 11:1-3 "… He said to them, "When you pray, say: 'Father, hallowed be your name, your kingdom come. Give us each day our daily bread."' We need to be asking God for our daily needs every day. Nothing should be taken for granted. God will meet all of our physical, emotional, and material needs, but He wants us to ask Him. That was what God was saying to me that day. I want things, but I don't come with the expectation that what I receive in return will meet my needs.

PRAY WITH DETERMINATION

Luke 11:5-8 says, "Then Jesus said to them, 'Suppose you have a friend, and you go to him at midnight and say, 'Friend, lend me three loaves of bread; a friend of mine on a journey has come to me, and I have no food to offer him.' And suppose the one inside answers, 'Don't bother me. The door is already locked, and my children and I are in bed. I can't get up and give you anything.' I tell you; even though He will not get up and give you the bread because of friendship, yet because of your *shameless audacity* He will surely get up and give you as much as you need.

"So I say to you: Ask and it will be given to you; seek and you will find; knock and the door will be opened to you. For everyone who asks receives; the one who seeks finds; and to the one who knocks, the door will be opened."

My son and daughter know how to play the system. They normally come to me when they want something and about half of the time, I say "no." Sometimes they get smart, and when I'm not in the room they ask my husband because, unlike me, more often than not he says yes. My kids know whom to ask to get what they want. Perhaps that is why we are told to enter the kingdom of God like a child; because your daddy gives you gifts as he deems fit. They don't have any fear or worry that they won't get it from their dad, because history has dictated that more often than not, they will get what they want from him if only they ask.

Do you pray like this? Do you pray with doubt that God will provide for your needs?

PRAY WITH SATISFACTION

Jesus Himself teaches us how to pray. When He prays in the garden, He says in Matthew 26:39, "My Father, if it is possible, may this cup be taken from me. Yet not as I will, but as you will." Jesus is not afraid to go to

His Daddy either. He minces no words, and tells God exactly what He wants. He prays God-sized prayers, too. But as much as it is the desire of His heart to not have to endure the pain of the cross, He also must know the purpose and reason behind His life on earth. Only a miracle would keep Him from having to go through this. He knew His father's heart and that God's will is that none should perish, but all should have eternal life. So, He prays with contentment. He prays "Not my will, but yours."

Do you pray with contentment that God's response to our prayers will benefit not only us, but will be in the best interest of the world?

9

The Power of Persistent Prayer

Getting to the heart of what it means to pray and trust.

by Debra Celovsky

Importune: to trouble with requests or demands; insistent; refusing to be denied

I sometimes find myself sitting with a woman who seems on the verge of being crushed under seemingly unbearable circumstances, wondering why her prayers remain unanswered. Empathetic answers and a shower of Scripture verses fall with little effect. Recently, I took a long look at a short parable in the Gospel of Luke. Within its eight short verses, a powerful man and a seemingly powerless woman face off in a test of wills. This test of wills, oddly enough, goes to the heart of what it means to pray—and trust—with absolute perseverance.

This small story told by Jesus appears between the mighty portrait of "as it was in the days of Noah," and the distinctive parable of the Pharisee and the tax collector. It may slip easily into the shadow of the other stories, but it shouldn't.

Jesus ministered during the rule of Herod Antipas, a son of the psychopathic Herod the Great. Justice in the courts was uneven at best during this rather lawless period. The social strata of that day dictated that the wealthy and powerful received swifter and, almost certainly, fairer justice from the legal system than the poor. The scenario, as presented by Jesus, would have been familiar to those who heard Him. But is He calling God unjust? Would He convey a picture of God as being irritated by the same day-after-day request of a desperate woman? No. In an intriguing twist, Jesus uses contrast rather than comparison to make two clear points: do not stop praying, for God will respond at precisely the right time. Do not lose heart, for God's delay is not God's denial.

THE STORY

A judge, with a reputation for arrogance and supreme self-confidence, is presented with the daily annoyance of a widow who has been wronged. His reputation is no secret. This would require her to embark on her mission knowing that a fair amount of verbal abuse would have to be endured. She would likely be repeatedly dismissed.

However, this knowledge did not rise to the level of her personal outrage. This widow has been badly, unjustly used. What are her options? She has no power, no social standing, and no other recourse. Ultimately, desperation and determination win out over the high probability of defeat. The judge, who "neither feared God, nor cared what people thought" was about to meet a resolute woman resolved to see her just claim satisfied.

The judge holds out on her for a time, Jesus tells the crowd that day. Yet for all his bluff and bluster, the judge actually takes some time to think about this aggravating situation: "Though I neither fear God nor respect man, yet because this widow keeps bothering me, I will give her justice, so that she will not beat me down by her continual coming" (Lk.18:4-5, ESV). The hammer of importunity has found a chink in the wall of implacability.

THE CONTRAST

If an obnoxious and unprincipled man will give in to the request of someone for whom he cares nothing (and who obviously annoys him), how much more will the Righteous One respond to those who are so dear to Him? This widow is a striking symbol of the people of God in desperate circumstances. She is a picture of hope driving a dogged request. Her only recourse is incessant petition. However, unlike the coarse and dismissive judge, our God is mightily pleased when we approach Him in confidence and resolute faith. Jesus uses the power of contrast to convey the boundless compassion of God. His eye on us is tender. We will not be turned away.

THE DELAY

At the same time, it is certain from our point of view that God does delay at times in answering our prayers. "How long, O Lord, how long?" This has often been the cry of the suffering, the martyrs, and the bereft throughout the ages. Delay is assuredly never due to God's absence or indifference or His unreadiness to help us. Rather, as much as we may resist the possibility, it may be our own unreadiness to receive the answer or the remedy God has in store for us.

"What does God want from this situation?" This can be a hard question to ask in the middle of extreme hardship. Our desire is to bring immediate relief to the woman in tough circumstances: abandoned or grieving or ill. But sometimes our responsibility is to encourage patient waiting and endurance. When relief comes, we may see far greater benefit from it. God is always at work on our faith, our character, and our future. Andrew Murray, in his classic little book, *With God in the School of Prayer*, writes: "Learn to give God time. He needs time with us . . . to exercise the full influence of His presence in us." That "full influence" is a lifelong process developed most intensely in seasons of adversity.

But in the parable, Jesus, who has such perfect insight into our nature, presses His point. When God does answer with mercy to His beloved and perhaps even judgment upon her adversaries, will we actually be expecting His response? Or will we, exhausted after long hope and expectation, be surprised by the manner of His solution? Will our attention be elsewhere? Jesus emphasizes that the answer, when it comes, may not be swift, but it might be sudden. Will He find our hearts still full of faith? This is an uncomfortable question, but Jesus is less interested in our comfort than our confidence in Him.

There is a terrific word picture in Psalm 97:2 where "righteousness and justice are the foundation of His throne." Not the armrests or the headrest or the beautiful adornments. No. They are the very elements upon which all other attributes of power rest.

So when we approach the throne of our God, in our powerlessness and great need, our eyes travel from the mighty, immovable bases of unfailing righteousness and sure justice to the face of a King who loves us.

Be encouraged to approach Him again and again, patiently, determinedly, and with absolute trust. There is no need to worry that it is a test of wills, as the little widow experienced. His pleasure is to hear us and answer with our greatest good in mind.

10

Scanning the Horizon

Help for when you're struggling to pray.

by Jill Briscoe

When you're struggling in your prayer life, make it
a habit to scan the horizon. Start looking around the
whole situation until you see a tiny answer to prayer.
Just a little one. Sometimes we get discouraged because
we don't think anything is happening unless there is
a storm-swept sky. We need to learn to discern the
approach of the blessing that God will surely send
our way. Look for the little things before the big
thing appears.

When Florence Nightingale went to the Crimean War
with her heroic band of nurses, she believed with all
her heart that God was sending them there. But when
they finally arrived after a horrendous journey, the
officer in charge tried to send them away. The soldiers
didn't want women around in that ghastly environment.
The nurses were confused and begged to stay and help,
but the soldiers were adamant. This was no place for
women, they said. The nurses prayed hard. It had been
incredibly difficult to get there. And they had been so
very sure God had sent them.

After a week or so, during which the camp commander refused to let the nurses do anything, Florence went to him and begged him to at least let them scrub the filthy floor of the makeshift hospital. He relented, but said, "Only the floor now, and then you have to go home."

The nurses rejoiced and got to work scrubbing the floor till it was spotless. They saw God's hand in this "small" answer to their prayers. They had seen a tiny cloud on the horizon, and they believed God for the rest. Sure enough, within a few days the camp commander allowed them to do another job and then another, until the sky became black with clouds and the rain finally came. These great women of God learned to scan the horizon for the smallest sign that the Lord was at work, and seeing that "small" cloud, they took courage to believe that God's full answer was on the way.

What is God asking you to pray for? Have you become discouraged by how few signs there are of His answer? Look up, scan the horizon. Watch for the little answers, and take heart. Soon the sky will be full of the evidence that God hears and answers prayer.

Author Biographies

Jill Briscoe is a popular writer and conference speaker who has authored over 50 books and travels all over the world. Jill is the founder of *Just Between Us*, a magazine encouraging and equipping women for a life of faith. Jill and her husband, Stuart, have been in ministry for over 50 years and have a worldwide radio ministry, *Telling the Truth*. She and her husband live in suburban Milwaukee, Wisconsin, have three grown children, and thirteen grandchildren.

Nancy J. Nordenson is a freelance writer with a specialty in medical writing. Nancy is the author of the book, *Women Who Think*. Married with two sons, she lives in Minneapolis, Minnesota, and is a member of the Evangelical Covenant Church denomination.

The late **Dr. Louis McBurney,** along with his wife, Melissa, cofounded Marble Retreat, a counseling center for clergy in the Colorado Rockies. It was started to help those in Christian ministry with the pressures they often experience. Dr. McBurney wrote numerous articles and books including: *Christian Sex Rules: A guide to what's allowed in the bedroom, Every Pastor Needs A Pastor, Counseling Christian Workers*, and many more.

Pamela S. Binkley has been involved in Bible Study Fellowship for 15 years. Studying Scripture is the passion of Pamela's life and watching others grow in spiritual maturity is her greatest joy. Pamela and her husband have been married almost 40 years and live in Houston, Texas. She has two grown children.

Sheila S. Hudson is the author of *13 Decisions That Will Change Your Life* and *13 Decisions That Will Transform Your Marriage*. She has also contributed to numerous other books. Sheila and her husband, Timothy, have worked in campus ministry for over 30 years and live in Athens, Georgia.

Shelly Esser has been the editor of *Just Between Us*, a magazine encouraging and equipping women for a life of faith, for over 25 years. She has written numerous articles and a book, and ministered to women for over 30 years. She and her husband live in southeastern Wisconsin. They have four daughters and two sons-in-laws.

Michelle Lazurek is an award-winning author, speaker, and pastor's wife. Additionally, she teaches at writers' conferences. Michelle lives in Wallingford, Connecticut.

Debra Celovsky is a freelance writer, and has served with her husband in pastoral ministry for 21 years. She has been involved in creating and teaching Bible studies, mentoring younger women, and traveling widely in missions. She and her husband have three grown children, and live in Santa Rosa, California.